Second Workshop on Multilingualism at the Intersection of Knowledge Bases and Machine Translation (MomenT-2019)

Held at Machine Translation Summit XVII

Dublin, Ireland
19-23 August 2019

ISBN: 978-1-5108-9249-1

Printed from e-media with permission by:

Curran Associates, Inc.
57 Morehouse Lane
Red Hook, NY 12571

Some format issues inherent in the e-media version may also appear in this print version.

Printed by Curran Associates, Inc. (2019)

For permission requests, please contact the Association for Computational Linguistics at the address below.

Association for Computational Linguistics
209 N. Eighth Street
Stroudsburg, Pennsylvania 18360

Phone: 1-570-476-8006
Fax: 1-570-476-0860

acl@aclweb.org

Additional copies of this publication are available from:

Curran Associates, Inc.
57 Morehouse Lane
Red Hook, NY 12571 USA
Phone: 845-758-0400
Fax: 845-758-2633
Email: curran@proceedings.com
Web: www.proceedings.com

Machine Translation Summit XVII

DUBLIN
MACHINE
TRANSLATION
SUMMIT 2019

MomenT-2019 – The Second Workshop on Multilingualism at the intersection of Knowledge Bases and Machine Translation

https://moment2019.insight-centre.org/

19–23 August, 2019
Dublin, Ireland

MomenT-2019 – The Second Workshop on Multilingualism at the intersection of Knowledge Bases and Machine Translation

https://moment2019.insight-centre.org/

19–23 August, 2019
Dublin, Ireland

Preface from the co-chairs of the workshop

The increasing availability of knowledge bases (KBs), generated by academia and industry, attracts the attentions of researchers in several natural language processing (NLP) tasks with the aim of advancing state-of-the-art performance by making use of the vast amount of background knowledge available in on the web. However, most of the information that is found in KBs, like knowledge graphs, ontologies or terminological resources, is represented, in most of the cases, in one language only (e.g. English, German or Italian). Consequently, NLP applications that use these KBs are therefore limited to the language in which the information is stored. To make the information accessible beyond language borders, these KBs have to be translated into different languages. Since a manual enhancement of KBs is a very time-consuming and expensive process, machine translation (MT) can be applied for this purpose. Nevertheless, this translation task with MT is rather challenging, due to the sophisticated information of a certain domain knowledge, documented in knowledge graphs, the specific vocabulary in terminological dictionaries and the particular sentence structure of ontology labels.

In addition to the multilingual enhancement of monolingual KBs, a growing attention has also been paid to the integration of existing multilingual terminological knowledge into MT systems or computer-assisted translation (CAT) tools. An important open issue for this task is how to support translators with relevant information when dealing with specialised texts from different domains (IT, medical, law, etc.). Commercial or open source MT systems trained on generic data are the most common solutions, but they often struggle with the translation of the specific vocabulary found in this task. To reduce the post-editing effort involved in the translation process, a valuable alternative is to enhance the systems with existing multilingual knowledge, e.g. IATE or in-house terminological resources, which are agreed and curated resources that professionals use in their expert-to-expert communication. In this sense, the provision of multilingual KBs, which could be better integrated into the MT systems is a crucial step towards increasing the translation quality, since terminological expressions are among the most common sources of translation errors.

Workshop organizers

Organizers

Workshop Chairs

Mihael Arcan	Insight Centre for Data Analytics, National University of Ireland Galway, Ireland
Marco Turchi	Fondazione Bruno Kessler (FBK), Italy
Jinhua Du	Investment AI, AIG, UK
Dimitar Shterionov	ADAPT Centre, Dublin City University, Ireland
Daniel Torregrosa	Insight Centre for Data Analytics, National University of Ireland Galway, Ireland

Program Committee

Eneko Agirre	University of the Basque Country
Juan Alberto Alonso	Lucy Software Ibérica SL
Alexandra Birch	The University of Edinburgh
Bram Bulte	Vrije Universiteit Brussel / VUB Centre for Linguistics (CLIN)
Christian Chiarcos	Goethe-Universität Frankfurt
Marta Ruiz Costa-jussà	Universitat Politècnica de Catalunya (UPC)
Béatrice Daille	Laboratoire d'Informatique Nantes Atlantique (LINA)
Thierry Declerck	Deutsches Forschungszentrum für Künstliche Intelligenz (DFKI GmbH)
Mauro Dragoni	Fondazione Bruno Kessler (FBK)
Tomaž Erjavec	Jožef Stefan Institute
Cristina España-Bonet	Saarland University / Deutsches Forschungszentrum für Künstliche Intelligenz (DFKI GmbH)
Christian Federmann	Microsoft
Natalia Grabar	STL CNRS Université Lille 3
Barry Haddow	The University of Edinburgh
Jochen Hummels	ESTeam
Miloš Jakubíček	Lexical Computing
Michael Jellinghaus	European Commission, DGT
Ilan Kernerman	K Dictionaries
Els Lefever	University College Ghent / Ghent University
Lieve Macken	Ghent University
Mirjam S. Maučec	University of Maribor
John P. McCrae	National University of Ireland, Galway
Johanna Monti	L'Orientale" University of Naples
Diego Moussallem	University of Paderborn
Roberto Navigli	Sapienza University of Rome
Matteo Negri	Fondazione Bruno Kessler (FBK)
Mariana Neves	German Federal Institute for Risk Assessment
Axel-Cyrille Ngonga Ngomo	Agile Knowledge Engineering and Semantic Web (AKSW)
Tony O'Dowd	KantanMT
Constantin Orasan	University of Wolverhampton
Marcis Pinnis	Tilde
Juan Pino	Facebook
Georg Rehm	Deutsches Forschungszentrum für Künstliche Intelligenz (DFKI GmbH)
Jean Senellart	SYSTRAN
Khalil Sima'an	Institute for Logic, Language and Computation, University of Amsterdam
Arda Tezcan	Ghent University
Josef van Genabith	Saarland University / Deutsches Forschungszentrum für Künstliche Intelligenz (DFKI GmbH)
Vincent Vandeghinste	Katholieke Universiteit Leuven
Špela Vintar	University of Ljubljana
Michał Ziemski	WIPO Translate

Contents

WordNet Gloss Translation for Under-resourced Languages using Multilingual Neural Machine Translation

Bharathi Raja Chakravarthi, Mihael Arcan, John P. McCrae
Insight Centre for Data Analytics
National University of Ireland Galway
Galway, Ireland
bharathi.raja@insight-centre.org,
mihael.arcan@insight-centre.org, john@mccr.ae

Abstract

In this paper, we translate the glosses in the English WordNet based on the expand approach for improving and generating wordnets with the help of multilingual neural machine translation. Neural Machine Translation (NMT) has recently been applied to many tasks in natural language processing, leading to state-of-the-art performance. However, the performance of NMT often suffers from low resource scenarios where large corpora cannot be obtained. Using training data from closely related language have proven to be invaluable for improving performance. In this paper, we describe how we trained multilingual NMT from closely related language utilizing phonetic transcription for Dravidian languages. We report the evaluation result of the generated wordnets sense in terms of precision. By comparing to the recently proposed approach, we show improvement in terms of precision.

1 Introduction

Wordnets are lexical resource organized as hierarchical structure based on synset and semantic features of the words (Miller, 1995; Fellbaum, 1998). Manually constructing wordnet is a difficult task and it takes years of experts' time. Another way is translating synsets of existing wordnet to the target language, then applying methods to identify exact matches or providing the translated synset to linguists and this has been proven to speed up wordnet creation. The latter approach is known as the *expand* approach. Popular wordnets like EuroWordNet (Vossen, 1997) and IndoWordNet (Bhattacharyya, 2010) were based on the *expand* approach. On the Global WordNet Association website,[1] a comprehensive list of wordnets available for different languages can be found, including IndoWordNet and EuroWordNet.

Due to the lack of parallel corpora, machine translation systems for less-resourced languages are not readily available. We attempt to utilize Multilingual Neural Machine Translation (MNMT) (Ha et al., 2016), where multiple sources and target languages are trained simultaneously without changes to the network architecture. This has been shown to improve the translation quality, however, most of the under-resourced languages use different scripts which limits the application of these multilingual NMT. In order to overcome this, we transliterate the languages on the target side and bring it into a single script to take advantage of multilingual NMT for closely-related languages. Closely-related languages refer to languages that share similar lexical and structural properties due to sharing a common ancestor (Popović et al., 2016). Frequently, languages in contact with other language or closely-related languages like the Dravidian, Indo-Aryan, and Slavic share words from a common root (*cognates*), which are highly semantically and phonologically similar.

In the scope of the wordnet creation for under-resourced languages, combining parallel corpus from closely related languages, phonetic transcription of the corpus and creating multilingual neural machine translation has been shown to improve the results in this paper. The evaluation results ob-

[1] http://globalwordnet.org/

tained from MNMT with transliterated corpus are better than the results of Statistical Machine Translation (SMT) from the recent work (Chakravarthi et al., 2018).

2 Related Work

The Princeton WordNet (Miller, 1995; Fellbaum, 1998) was built from scratch. The taxonomies of the languages, synsets, relations among synset are built first in the merge approach. Popular wordnets like EuroWordNet (Vossen, 1997) and IndoWordNet (Bhattacharyya, 2010) are developed by the expand approach whereby the synsets are built in correspondence with the existing wordnet synsets by translation. For the Tamil language, Rajendran et al. (2002) proposed a design template for the Tamil wordnet.

To evaluate and improve the wordnets for the targeted under-resourced Dravidian languages, Chakravarthi et al. (2018) followed the approach of Arcan et al. (2016), which uses the existing translations of wordnets in other languages to identify contextual information for wordnet senses from a large set of generic parallel corpora. They use this contextual information to improve the translation quality of WordNet senses. They showed that their approach can help overcome the drawbacks of simple translations of words without context. Chakravarthi et al. (2018) removed the code-mixing based on the script of the parallel corpus to reduce the noise in translation. The authors used the SMT to create bilingual MT for three Dravidian languages. In our work, we use MNMT system and we transliterate the closely related language corpus into a single script to take advantage of MNMT systems.

Neural Machine Translation achieved rapid development in recent years, however, conventional NMT (Bahdanau et al., 2015) creates a separate machine translation system for each pair of languages. Creating individual machine translation system for many languages is resource consuming, considering there are around 7000 languages in the world. Recent work on NMT, specifically on low-resource (Zoph et al., 2016; Chen et al., 2017) or zero-resource machine translation (Johnson et al., 2017; Firat et al., 2016) uses third languages as pivots and showed that translation quality is significantly improved. Ha et al. (2016) proposed an approach to extend the Bahdanau et al. (2015) architecture to multilingual translation by sharing the entire model. The approach of shared vocabulary across multiple languages resulted in a shared embedding space. Although the results were promising, the result of the experiments was reported in highly resourced languages such as English, German, and French but many under-resourced languages have different syntax and semantic structure to these languages. Chakravarthi et al. (2019) shown that using languages belonging to the same family and phonetic transcription of parallel corpus to a single script improves the MNMT results.

Our approach extends that of Chakravarthi et al. (2019) and Chakravarthi et al. (2018) by utilizing MNMT with a transliterated parallel corpus of closely related languages to create wordnet sense for Dravidian languages. In particular, we downloaded the data, removed code-mixing and phonetically transcribed each corpus to Latin script. Two types of experiments were performed: In the first one, where we just removed code-mixing and compiled the multilingual corpora by concatenating the parallel corpora from three languages. In the second one removed code-mixing, phonetically transcribed the corpora and then compiled the multilingual corpora by concatenating the parallel corpora from three languages. These two experiments are contribution to this work compared to the previous works.

3 Experiment Setup

3.1 Dravidian Languages

For our study, we perform experiments on Tamil (ISO 639-1: ta), Telugu (ISO 639-1: te) and Kannada (ISO 639-1: kn). The targeted languages for this work differ in their orthographies due to historical reasons and whether they adopted the Sanskrit tradition or not (Bhanuprasad and Svenson, 2008). Each of these has been assigned a unique block in Unicode, and thus from an MNMT perspective are completely distinct.

3.2 Multilingual Neural Machine Translation

Johnson et al. (2017) and Ha et al. (2016) extended the architecture of Bahdanau et al. (2015) to use a universal model to handle multiple source and target languages with a special tag in the encoder to determine which target language to translate. The idea is to use the unified vocabulary and training corpus without modification in the architecture to take advantage of the shared embedding. The goal of this approach is to improve the translation quality for individual languages pairs, for which parallel corpus data is scarce by letting the NMT to learn the common semantics across languages and reduce the number of translation systems needed. The sentence of different languages are distinguished through languages codes.

3.3 Data

We used datasets from Chakravarthi et al. (2018) in our experiment. The authors collected three Dravidian languages $\leftrightarrow$ English pairs from OPUS[2] web-page (Tiedemann and Nygaard, 2004). Corpus statistics are shown in Table 1. More descriptions about the three datasets can be found in Chakravarthi et al. (2018). We transliterated this corpus using Indic-trans library[3]. All the sentences are first tokenized with OpenNMT (Klein et al., 2017) tokenizer and then segmented into subword symbols using Byte Pair Encoding (BPE) (Sennrich et al., 2016). We learn the BPE merge operations across all the languages. Following Ha et al. (2016), we indicate the language by prepending two tokens to indicate the desired source and target language. An example of a sentence in English to be translated into Tamil would be:

```
src__en tgt_ta I like ice-cream
```

3.4 Transliteration

As the Indian languages under our study are written in different scripts, they must be converted to some common representation before training the MNMT to take advantage of closely related language resources. A phonetic transcription is an approach where a word in one script is transformed into a different script by maintaining phonetic correspondence. Phonetic transcribing to Latin script and International Phonetic Alphabet (IPA) was studied by (Chakravarthi et al., 2019) and showed that Latin script outperforms IPA for the MNMT Dravidian languages. The improvements in results were shown in terms of the BLEU (Papineni et al., 2002), METEOR (Banerjee and Lavie, 2005) and chrF (Popović, 2015) metric. To evaluate the similarity of the corpus the authors used cosine similarity and shown that transcribing to Latin script retain more similarity. We used Indic-trans library by Bhat et al. (2015), which bring all the languages into a single representation by phoneme matching algorithm. The same library can also back-transliterate from English (Latin script) to Indian languages.

3.5 Code-Mixing

Code-mixing is a phenomenon which occurs commonly in most multilingual societies where the speaker or writer alternate between two or more languages in a sentence (Ayeomoni, 2006; Ranjan et al., 2016; Yoder et al., 2017; Parshad et al., 2016). Since most of our corpus came from publicly available parallel corpus are created by voluntary annotators or align automatically. The technical documents translation such as KDE, GNOME, and Ubuntu translations have code-mixing data since some of the technical terms may not be known to voluntary annotators for translation. But the code-mixing from OpenSubtitle are due to bilingual and historical reasons of Indian speakers (Chanda et al., 2016; Parshad et al., 2016). Different combinations of languages may occur while code-mixing for example German-Italian and French-Italian in Switzerland, Hindi-Telugu in state of Telangana, India, Taiwanese-Mandarin Chinese in Taiwan (Chan et al., 2009). Since the Internet era, English become the international language of the younger generation. Hence, English words are frequently embedded in Indians' speech. For our work, only intra-sentential code-mixing was taken into account. In this case, Dravidian languages as the primary language, and English as secondary languages. We removed the English words considering only the English as a foreign word based on the script. Statistics of the removal of code-mixing is shown in Table 2.

3.6 WordNet creation

Using contextual information to improve the translation quality of wordnet senses was shown to improve the results (Arcan et al., 2016). The approach is to select the most relevant sentences from a parallel corpus based on the overlap of existing wordnet translations. For each synset of wordnet entry, multiple sentences were collected that share semantic information. We use this contextual data in English to be translated into Tamil, Telugu, and Kannada using our MNMT system.

4 Results

We present consolidated results in Table 3. Apart from Precision at 1, the Table 3 shows Precision at 2, Precision at 5, Precision at 10. The goal of

[2]http://opus.nlpl.eu/

[3]https://github.com/libindic/indic-trans

	English-Tamil		English-Telugu		English-Kannada	
	English	Tamil	English	Telugu	English	Kannada
Number of tokens	7,738,432	6,196,245	258,165	226,264	68,197	71,697
Number of unique words	134,486	459,620	18,455	28,140	7,740	15,683
Average word length	4.2	7.0	3.7	4.8	4.5	6.0
Average sentence length	5.2	7.9	4.6	5.6	5.3	6.8
Number of sentences	449,337		44,588		13,543	

Table 1: Statistics of the parallel corpora used to train the translation systems.

	English-Tamil		English-Telugu		English-Kannada	
	English	Tamil	English	Telugu	English	Kannada
tok	0.5% (45,847)	1.1% (72,833)	2.8% (7,303)	4.9% (12,818)	3.5% (2,425)	9.0% (6,463)
sent	0.9% (4,100)		3.1% (1,388)		3.4% (468)	

Table 2: Number of sentences (sent) and number of tokens (tok) removed from the original corpus.

this work is to aid the human annotator in speeding up the process of wordnet creation for under-resourced languages. Precision at different levels is calculated by comparing it with IndoWordNet for the exact match out of the top 10 words from word alignment based on the attention model in MNMT and alignment from SMT. The precision of all the MNMT systems is greater than the baseline.

The perfect match of a word and IndoWordNet entry is considered for Precision at 1. Tamil, Telugu, and Kannada yield better precision at a different level for translation based on both MNMT. For Tamil and Telugu, the translation based on MNMT trained on the native script and MNMT trained on transcribed script did not have much variance. The slight reduction in the result is caused by the transliteration into and back to the original script. In the case of Kannada, which has very less number of parallel sentences to train compared to the other two languages, the MNMT translation trained on transcribed script shows high improvement.

We have several observations. First, the precision presented is below 15 percent and this is because these languages have very minimum parallel corpora. Chakravarthi et al. (2018) used the corpora collected during August 2017 from OPUS which contains mostly translation of religious text, technical document, and subtitles. Analyzing the results by comparing with IndoWordNet is likely to be problematic since it is far from complete and is overly skewed to the classical words for these languages. Second, our method outperforms the baseline from (Chakravarthi et al., 2018) for all the languages, demonstrating the effectiveness of our framework for multilingual NMT. More

	English→Tamil			
	P@10	P@5	P@2	P@1
B-SMT	0.1200	0.1087	0.0833	0.0651
NC-SMT	0.1252	0.1147	0.0911	0.0725
NC-MNMT	**0.2030**	**0.1559**	0.1228	0.1161
NCT-MNMT	0.1816	0.1538	**0.1351**	**0.1320**
	English→Telugu			
	P@10	P@5	P@2	P@1
B-SMT	0.0471	0.0455	0.0380	0.0278
NC-SMT	0.0467	0.0451	0.0382	0.0274
NC-MNMT	**0.0933**	0.0789	0.0509	0.0400
NCT-MNMT	0.0918	**0.0807**	**0.0599**	**0.0565**
	English→Kannada			
	P@10	P@5	P@2	P@1
B-SMT	0.0093	0.0096	0.0080	0.0055
NC-SMT	0.0110	0.0107	0.0091	0.0067
NC-MNMT	0.0652	0.0472	0.0319	0.0226
NCT-MNMT	**0.0906**	**0.0760**	**0.0535**	**0.0433**

Table 3: Results of Automatic evaluation of translated wordnet with IndoWordNet Precision at different level denoted by P@10 which means Precision at 10. B-Baseline original corpus, NC- Non-code mixed, MNMT-Multilingual Neural Machine Translation, NCT-MNMT Multilingual Neural Machine Translation

importantly, transliterating the parallel corpora is more beneficial for the low resource language pair English-Kannada.

Manual Evaluation

In order to re-confirm the validity of the output in practical scenarios, we also performed a human-based evaluation in comparison with IndoWordNet entries. For human evaluation 50 wordnet entries from the wordnet were randomly selected. All these entries were evaluated according to the manual evaluation method performed by Chakravarthi et al. (2018). The classification from the paper is given below. More details about the classification

	B-SMT	NC-SMT	NC-MNMT	NC-MNMT-T
Agrees with IndoWordNet	18%	20%	**28%**	26%
Inflected form	12%	22%	26%	**30%**
Transliteration	4%	4%	2%	2%
Spelling variant	2%	2%	2%	2%
Correct, but not in IndoWordNet	18%	**24%**	22%	**24%**
Incorrect	46%	28%	20%	**16%**

Table 4: Manual evaluation of wordnet creation for Tamil language compared with IndoWordNet (IWN) at precision at 10 presented in percentage. B-Baseline original corpus, NC- Non-code mixed, MNMT-Multilingual Neural Machine Translation, NCT-MNMT Multilingual Neural Machine Translation

can be found in Chakravarthi et al. (2018).

- **Agrees with IndoWordNet** Perfect match with IndoWordNet.
- **Inflected form** Some parts of a word such root of a word is found.
- **Transliteration** Transliteration of an English word in Tamil this might be due to unavailability of the translation in the parallel corpus.
- **Spelling Variant** Spelling variant can be caused by wrong or misspelling of the word according to IndoWordNet. Since the corpus contains data from OpenSubtitle this might include dialect variation of the word.
- **Correct, but not in IndoWordNet** Word sense not found in IndoWordNet but found in our translation. We verified we had identified the correct sense by referring to the wordnet gloss.
- **Incorrect** This error class can be caused due to inappropriate term or mistranslated.

Table 4 contains the percentage for outputs of the wordnet translation. As mentioned earlier in Section 3, SMT systems trained on removing code-mixing and without removing are used as baselines for this assessment. The baseline system shows that the cleaned data (removing code-mix) produce better results. Again, as we previously mentioned both our MNMT system trained on cleaned data are better than the baseline system in the manual evaluation as well. From Table 4, we can see that there is a significant improvement over the inflected form MNMT systems trained with the transcribed corpus. Perfect match with IndoWordNet is lower for MNMT trained with transcribed corpus compared to MNMT trained on the original script but still better than the baselines. This might be due to back-transliteration effect. It is clear from the results that this translation can be used as an aid by annotators to create wordnet for under-resourced languages.

5 Conclusion

In this paper, we presented how to take advantage of phonetic transcription and multilingual NMT to improve the wordnet sense translation of under-resourced languages. The proposed approach incorporates code-mixing phenomenon into consideration as well as the phonetic transcription of closely related language to better utilize multilingual NMT. We evaluated the proposed approach on three Dravidian languages and showed that the proposed approach outperforms the baseline by effectively leveraging the information from closely related languages. Moreover, our approach can provide better translations for very low resourced language pair (English-Kannada). In the future, we would like to conduct an experiment by transcribing the languages to one of the Dravidian languages scripts which will be able to represent information more easily than Latin script.

Acknowledgments

This work is supported by a research grant from Science Foundation Ireland, co-funded by the European Regional Development Fund, for the Insight Centre under Grant Number SFI/12/RC/2289 and the European Union's Horizon 2020 research and innovation programme under grant agreement No 731015, ELEXIS - European Lexical Infrastructure and grant agreement No 825182, Prêt-à-LLOD.

References

Arcan, Mihael, John P. McCrae, and Paul Buitelaar. 2016. Expanding wordnets to new languages with multilingual sense disambiguation. In *Proceedings of The 26th International Conference on Computational Linguistics*.

Ayeomoni, Moses Omoniyi. 2006. Code-switching and code-mixing: Style of language use in childhood in Yoruba speech community. *Nordic Journal of African Studies*, 15(1):90–99.

Bahdanau, Dzmitry, Kyunghyun Cho, and Yoshua Bengio. 2015. Neural machine translation by jointly learning to align and translate. In *3rd International Conference on Learning Representations, ICLR 2015, San Diego, CA, USA, May 7-9, 2015, Conference Track Proceedings*.

Banerjee, Satanjeev and Alon Lavie. 2005. METEOR: An Automatic Metric for MT Evaluation with Improved Correlation with Human Judgments. In *Proceedings of the ACL Workshop on Intrinsic and Extrinsic Evaluation Measures for Machine Translation and/or Summarization*, pages 65–72. Association for Computational Linguistics.

Bhanuprasad, Kamadev and Mats Svenson. 2008. Errgrams - A Way to Improving ASR for Highly Inflected Dravidian Languages. In *Proceedings of the Third International Joint Conference on Natural Language Processing: Volume-II*.

Bhat, Irshad Ahmad, Vandan Mujadia, Aniruddha Tammewar, Riyaz Ahmad Bhat, and Manish Shrivastava. 2015. IIIT-H System Submission for FIRE2014 Shared Task on Transliterated Search. In *Proceedings of the Forum for Information Retrieval Evaluation*, FIRE '14, pages 48–53, New York, NY, USA. ACM.

Bhattacharyya, Pushpak. 2010. IndoWordNet. In Chair), Nicoletta Calzolari (Conference, Khalid Choukri, Bente Maegaard, Joseph Mariani, Jan Odijk, Stelios Piperidis, Mike Rosner, and Daniel Tapias, editors, *Proceedings of the Seventh International Conference on Language Resources and Evaluation (LREC'10)*, Valletta, Malta, May. European Language Resources Association (ELRA).

Chakravarthi, Bharathi Raja, Mihael Arcan, and John P. McCrae. 2018. Improving Wordnets for Under-Resourced Languages Using Machine Translation. In *Proceedings of the 9th Global WordNet Conference*. The Global WordNet Conference 2018 Committee.

Chakravarthi, Bharathi Raja, Mihael Arcan, and John P. McCrae. 2019. Comparison of Different Orthographies for Machine Translation of Under-resourced Dravidian Languages. In *Proceedings of the 2nd Conference on Language, Data and Knowledge*.

Chan, Joyce Y. C., Houwei Cao, P. C. Ching, and Tan Lee. 2009. Automatic Recognition of Cantonese-English Code-Mixing Speech. In *International Journal of Computational Linguistics & Chinese Language Processing, Volume 14, Number 3, September 2009*, September.

Chanda, Arunavha, Dipankar Das, and Chandan Mazumdar. 2016. Columbia-Jadavpur submission for emnlp 2016 code-switching workshop shared task: System description. *EMNLP 2016*, page 112.

Chen, Yun, Yang Liu, Yong Cheng, and Victor O.K. Li. 2017. A Teacher-Student Framework for Zero-Resource Neural Machine Translation. In *Proceedings of the 55th Annual Meeting of the Association for Computational Linguistics (Volume 1: Long Papers)*, pages 1925–1935. Association for Computational Linguistics.

Fellbaum, Christiane, editor. 1998. *WordNet: an electronic lexical database*. MIT Press.

Firat, Orhan, Baskaran Sankaran, Yaser Al-Onaizan, Fatos T. Yarman Vural, and Kyunghyun Cho. 2016. Zero-Resource Translation with Multi-Lingual Neural Machine Translation. In *Proceedings of the 2016 Conference on Empirical Methods in Natural Language Processing*, pages 268–277. Association for Computational Linguistics.

Ha, Thanh-Le, Jan Niehues, and Alexander H. Waibel. 2016. Toward multilingual neural machine translation with universal encoder and decoder. In *Proceedings of the International Workshop on Spoken Language Translation*.

Johnson, Melvin, Mike Schuster, Quoc V. Le, Maxim Krikun, Yonghui Wu, Zhifeng Chen, Nikhil Thorat, Fernanda Viégas, Martin Wattenberg, Greg Corrado, Macduff Hughes, and Jeffrey Dean. 2017. Google's multilingual neural machine translation system: Enabling zero-shot translation. *Transactions of the Association for Computational Linguistics*, 5:339–351, December.

Klein, Guillaume, Yoon Kim, Yuntian Deng, Jean Senellart, and Alexander Rush. 2017. OpenNMT: Open-Source Toolkit for Neural Machine Translation. In *Proceedings of ACL 2017, System Demonstrations*, pages 67–72. Association for Computational Linguistics.

Miller, George A. 1995. WordNet: a lexical database for English. *Communications of the ACM*, 38(11):39–41.

Papineni, Kishore, Salim Roukos, Todd Ward, and Wei-Jing Zhu. 2002. BLEU: a Method for Automatic Evaluation of Machine Translation. In *Proceedings of the 40th Annual Meeting of the Association for Computational Linguistics*.

Parshad, Rana D., Suman Bhowmick, Vineeta Chand, Nitu Kumari, and Neha Sinha. 2016. What is India speaking? Exploring the "Hinglish" invasion. *Physica A: Statistical Mechanics and its Applications*, 449:375 – 389.

Popović, Maja, Mihael Arcan, and Filip Klubička. 2016. Language Related Issues for Machine Translation between Closely Related South Slavic Languages. In *Proceedings of the Third Workshop on NLP for Similar Languages, Varieties and Dialects (VarDial3)*, pages 43–52. The COLING 2016 Organizing Committee.

Popović, Maja. 2015. chrF: character n-gram F-score for automatic MT evaluation. In *Proceedings of the Tenth Workshop on Statistical Machine Translation*, pages 392–395. Association for Computational Linguistics.

Rajendran, S, S Arulmozi, B Kumara Shanmugam, S Baskaran, and S Thiagarajan. 2002. Tamil WordNet. In *Proceedings of the First International Global WordNet Conference. Mysore*, volume 152, pages 271–274.

Ranjan, Prakash, Bharathi Raja, Ruba Priyadharshini, and Rakesh Chandra Balabantaray. 2016. A comparative study on code-mixed data of Indian social media vs formal text. In *2nd International Conference on Contemporary Computing and Informatics (IC3I)*, pages 608–611. IEEE.

Tiedemann, Jorg and Lars Nygaard. 2004. The OPUS Corpus - Parallel and Free: http://logos.uio.no/opus . In *Proceedings of the Fourth International Conference on Language Resources and Evaluation (LREC'04)*. European Language Resources Association (ELRA).

Vossen, Piek. 1997. EuroWordNet: a multilingual database for information retrieval. In *In: Proceedings of the DELOS workshop on Cross-language Information Retrieval*, pages 5–7.

Yoder, Michael, Shruti Rijhwani, Carolyn Rosé, and Lori Levin. 2017. Code-Switching as a Social Act: The Case of Arabic Wikipedia Talk Pages. In *Proceedings of the Second Workshop on NLP and Computational Social Science*, pages 73–82. Association for Computational Linguistics.

Zoph, Barret, Deniz Yuret, Jonathan May, and Kevin Knight. 2016. Transfer Learning for Low-Resource Neural Machine Translation. In *Proceedings of the 2016 Conference on Empirical Methods in Natural Language Processing*, pages 1568–1575. Association for Computational Linguistics.

Leveraging SNOMED CT terms and relations for machine translation of clinical texts from Basque to Spanish

Xabier Soto, Olatz Perez-de-Viñaspre, Maite Oronoz, Gorka Labaka
Ixa Research Group, University of the Basque Country (UPV/EHU)
{xabier.soto, olatz.perezdevinaspre, maite.oronoz, gorka.labaka}@ehu.eus

Abstract

We present a method for machine translation of clinical texts without using bilingual clinical texts, leveraging the rich terminology and structure of the Systematized Nomenclature of Medicine – Clinical Terms (SNOMED CT), which is considered the most comprehensive, multilingual clinical health care terminology collection in the world. We evaluate our method for Basque to Spanish translation, comparing the performance with and without using clinical domain resources. As a method to leverage domain-specific knowledge, we incorporate to the training corpus lexical bilingual resources previously used for the automatic translation of SNOMED CT into Basque, as well as artificial sentences created making use of the relations specified in SNOMED CT. Furthermore, we use available Electronic Health Records in Spanish for backtranslation and copying. For assessing our proposal, we use Recurrent Neural Network and Transformer architectures, and we try diverse techniques for backtranslation, using not only Neural Machine Translation but also Rule-Based and Statistical Machine Translation systems. We observe large and consistent improvements ranging from 10 to 15 BLEU points, obtaining the best automatic evaluation results using Transformer for both general architecture and backtranslation systems.

1 Introduction

The objective of this work is to study the utility of available clinical domain resources in a real use-case, which is the translation of Electronic Health Records (EHR) from Basque to Spanish. Basque is a minoritised language, also in the Basque public health service, where most of the EHRs are written in Spanish so that any doctor can understand them. With the aim of enabling Basque speaking doctors to write EHRs in Basque, we have the long-term objective of developing machine translation systems to translate clinical texts between Basque and Spanish. This work presents a method for machine translation of clinical texts from Basque to Spanish, conditioned by the current lack of clinical domain corpora in Basque.

Neural Machine Translation (NMT) has become in the past recent years the prevailing technology for machine translation, especially in the research community. Several architectures have been proposed for NMT, ranging from the initial Convolutional Neural Networks (CNN) (Kalchbrenner and Blunsom, 2013) and Recurrent Neural Networks (RNN) (Sutskever et al., 2014), to the most advanced Transformer (Vaswani et al., 2017). However, it is known that NMT systems require a large amount of training data to obtain optimal results (Koehn and Knowles, 2017), so traditional techniques as Rule-Based Machine Translation (RBMT) and Statistical Machine Translation (SMT) (Koehn et al., 2003) can be considered when the available resources are low.

One of the techniques that has become a standard to increase the available resources for NMT systems is backtranslation (Sennrich et al., 2015a), consisting in automatically translating a monolingual corpus from the target language into the source language, and then adding both original and translated corpora to the training corpus. In our case, the availability of EHRs in Spanish enables us to improve the results for the translation of clinical texts from Basque to Spanish, also serving us as a resource for domain adaptation.

Another of our challenges is to study how to translate clinical text, which has its own characteristics differentiated from texts from other domains. Usually, the grammar of the sentences in EHRs is simplified, often omitting verbs, missing punctuation, using many acronyms and with a non-standard language more oriented to communicate between doctors than for being understood by patients. Furthermore, the main difficulty of translating clinical texts comes from the rich vocabulary used in EHRs to refer to drugs, diseases, body parts and other clinical terminology.

Regarding the language pair, our main challenge is to deal with long distance languages as Basque and Spanish, with the complexity associated with it. Specifically, we have to address the challenge of translating from a language with the characteristics of Basque. Briefly, Basque language can be described as a highly agglutinative language, with a rich morphology, where words are usually created adding diverse suffixes that mark different cases. The morphology of verbs is especially complex, including morphemes that add information about the subject, object, number, tense, aspect, etc. It is thought that the BPE word segmentation commonly used in NMT (Sennrich et al., 2015b), originally developed for avoiding the out-of-vocabulary problem, is also beneficial for the translation from morphologically rich languages as Basque.

2 Related work

Several approaches have been tried for machine translation of Basque, including Example-Based (Stroppa et al., 2006), Rule-Based (Mayor, 2007) and Statistical systems (Labaka, 2010). First works have been published for Neural Machine Translation of Basque (Etchegoyhen et al., 2018; Jauregi et al., 2018), and the first general domain commercial system for NMT between Basque and Spanish is already available online.[1]

In the NMT approach for Basque by Etchegoyhen et al. (2018), diverse morphological segmentation techniques are tested, including the aforementioned Byte Pair Encoding (BPE) (Sennrich et al., 2015b), the linguistically motivated vocabulary reduction originally proposed for Turkish (Ataman et al., 2017) and the ixaKat morphological analyser for Basque (Alegria et al., 1996; Otegi et al., 2016). They also tried character-based Machine Translation (Lee et al., 2016), obtaining the best results for translating from Basque to Spanish when applying the morphological analyser for Basque followed by BPE word segmentation to the source language corpus, and only BPE word segmentation to the target language corpus.

Regarding the clinical domain, Perez-de-Vinaspre (2017) developed a system for automatically translating the clinical terminology included in SNOMED CT (IHTSDO, 2014) into Basque. Perez-de-Vinaspre (2017) combined the use of lexical resources, transliteration of neoclassic terms, generation of nested terms and the adaptation of a RBMT system for the medical domain as backup. With respect to the translation of EHRs, the bibliography is scarce, and nowadays we can only refer to a preliminary study for translating clinical notes from English to Spanish (Liu and Cai, 2015).

Another approach for the task of translation of clinical texts is domain adaptation. Usually, when low resources for the desired domain are available, a bigger corpus from another domain is used to first train the system, which is then fine-tuned with the available in-domain corpus (Zoph et al., 2016). From another point of view, Bapna and Firat (2019) try to combine non-parametric or retrieval based approaches with NMT, looking for similarities between n-grams in the sentence to be translated and part of previously translated sentences, and then using this information for producing more accurate translations.

Concerning backtranslation, we have considered the analysis performed by Poncelas et al. (2018), where different sizes of backtranslated corpora were added to the human translated corpora used as training corpus; and regarding the techniques used for backtranslation, we follow the work by Burlot and Yvon (2019) in which they compare the performance of different SMT and NMT systems for this task.

3 Resources and methodology

As mentioned in the introduction, our main handicap is the lack of clinical domain bilingual corpora. To overcome this, we make use of available out-

[1] `https://www.modela.eus/eu/itzultzailea` (Accessed on April 11, 2019.)

of-domain bilingual corpora, automatically created clinical terminology in Basque (Perez-de-Viñaspre, 2017), artificial sentences formed based on the relations specified in SNOMED CT, and EHRs in Spanish that are used for backtranslation (Sennrich et al., 2015a) and copying (Currey et al., 2017).

For evaluation in the clinical domain, we use EHR templates in Basque published with academic purposes (Joanes Etxeberri Saria V. Edizioa, 2014), together with their manual translations into Spanish performed by a bilingual doctor.

In the following, we present the details of each of the resources and explain how they were used in this work.

3.1 Out-of-domain corpora

As a basis for our work, we use a large bilingual corpus formed by 4.5 million sentences, where 2.3 million sentences are a repetition of a corpus from the news domain (Etchegoyhen et al., 2016), and the remaining 2.2 million sentences are from diverse domains such as administrative, web-crawling and specialised magazines (consumerism and science). These corpora were compiled from sources such as EITB (Basque public broadcaster), Elhuyar (research foundation) and IVAP (Basque institute of public administration).

3.2 Clinical terminology

As a first step for improving the translation of clinical texts, we built a dictionary with all the Basque terms and their corresponding Spanish entries used for the automatic translation of SNOMED CT into Basque (Perez-de-Viñaspre, 2017). These terms were compiled from different sources such as Euskalterm, Elhuyar Science and Technology dictionary, UPV/EHU human anatomy atlas and nursery dictionary, International Classification of Diseases dictionary and a health administration related dictionary. As this work corresponds to a first approach of developing a Basque version of SNOMED CT, more than a possible Basque term was created for each entry in Spanish. Altogether, we use 151,111 Basque terms corresponding to 83,360 unique Spanish terms. We think that the fact of having more than one possible Basque term for each Spanish entry helps us to improve the coverage of the system for translating from Basque to Spanish. As a sample, Table 1 shows the first 10 clinical terms included as training corpus.

3.3 Artificial sentences

While including clinical terms in our system helps us to approach the rich terminology characteristic of clinical notes, we think that including these same terms in the form of sentences could be more suitable to the task of translating sentences from EHRs. For doing this, we leverage the structured form of SNOMED CT, using the relations specified in it to create simple artificial sentences that could be more similar to the real sentences included in EHRs.

Specifically, the Snapshot release of the international version on RF2 format of the SNOMED CT delivery from 31st July 2017 was used. For the sentences to be representative, the most frequent active relations were taken into account, only considering the type of relations that appeared more than 10,000 times. The most frequent active relations in the used version were "is a", "finding site", "associated morphology" and "method".

For creating the artificial sentences, we first defined two sentence models for each of the most

Basque term	Spanish term	English gloss
organo kopulatzaile	órgano copulador	*copulatory organ*
dionisiako	dionisiaco	*Dionysian*
desfile	desfile	*parade*
begi-miiasia	miasis ocular	*ophthalmic myiasis*
ahoko kandidiasi	candidiasis oral	*oral candidiasis*
wolfram	wolframio	*Tungsten*
W	wolframio	*Tungsten*
zergari	recaudador	*collector*
jasotzaile	recaudador	*collector*
biltzaile	recaudador	*collector*

Table 1: First 10 clinical terms included as training corpus.

frequent relations in SNOMED CT. Taking these sentence models as a reference, for each of the concepts concerning a unique pair of Basque and Spanish terms, we randomly chose one of the relations that this concept has in SNOMED CT. When doing this, we restricted the possible relations to the most frequent ones and omitted the relations with terms that were not available in both languages. Finally, we randomly chose one of the two sentence models for this specific relation.

Considering the agglutinative character of Basque language, some of the created sentences needed the application of morphological inflections to the specific terms included in the artificial sentences. For this task, a transducer was applied following the inflection rules defined in the Xuxen spelling corrector (Agirre et al., 1992). In total, 363,958 sentences were created. As a sample, Table 2 shows the first 10 artificial sentences created with this method, separating different terms and relations with '|', giving the same superscript number to equivalent terms, and marking the terms that define the relations in bold.

3.4 EHRs in Spanish

Finally, as a main contribution to the translation of clinical texts, we make use of available EHRs in Spanish. This corpus is made up of real health records from the hospital of Galdakao-Usansolo consisting of 142,154 documents compiled from

<table>
<tr><th>Basque sentence</th><th>Spanish sentence</th></tr>
<tr><td>umetokiaren prolapsoa^1 | emakumezkoaren prolapso genitala, zehaztugabea^2 | da
uterine prolapse^1 | is a | prolapse of female genital organs, undefined^2</td><td>prolapso uterino^1 | es | prolapso de los órganos genitales femeninos^2
uterine prolapse^1 | is a | prolapse of female genital organs^2</td></tr>
<tr><td>umetokiaren prolapsoa^1 | uteroa^2 | -n gertatzen da
uterine prolapse^1 | occurs in | uterus^2</td><td>descenso uterino^1 | ocurre en | estructura uterina^2
descensus uteri^1 | occurs in | uterine structure^2</td></tr>
<tr><td>umetokiaren prolapsoa^1 | uteroaren egitura^2 | -n aurkitzen da
uterine prolapse^1 | is found in | uterine structure^2</td><td>hernia uterina^1 | se encuentra en | estructura uterina^2
uterine hernia^1 | is found in | uterine structure^2</td></tr>
<tr><td>uteroaren prolapsoa^1 | emakumezkoaren prolapso genitala, zehaztugabea^2 | da
uterine prolapse^1 | is a | prolapse of female genital organs, undefined^2</td><td>prolapso uterino^1 | es | prolapso genital^2
uterine prolapse^1 | is a | genital prolapse^2</td></tr>
<tr><td>uteroaren prolapsoa^1 | umetokiko trastorno ez-inflamatorioa, zehaztugabea^2 | mota bat da
uterine prolapse^1 | is a type of | noninflammatory uterine disorder, undefined^2</td><td>descenso uterino^1 | es un tipo de | trastorno uterino^2
descensus uteri^1 | is a type of | uterine disorder^2</td></tr>
<tr><td>uteroaren prolapsoa^1 | umetokiaren nahasmendua^2 | da
uterine prolapse^1 | is a | uterine disorder^2</td><td>hernia uterina^1 | es | enfermedad uterina^2
uterine hernia^1 | is a | uterine disease^2</td></tr>
<tr><td>zakilaren inflamazioa^1 | zakil^2 | -ean gertatzen da
inflammation of penis^1 | occurs in | penis^2</td><td>inflamación del pene^1 | ocurre en | estructura de pene^2
inflammation of penis^1 | occurs in | penis structure^2</td></tr>
<tr><td>zakilaren inflamazioa^1 | zakilaren egitura^2 | -n aurkitzen da
inflammation of penis^1 | is found in | penis structure^2</td><td>trastorno inflamatorio del pene^1 | se encuentra en | pene^2
inflammatory disorder of penis^1 | is found in | penis^2</td></tr>
<tr><td>zakilaren hantura^1 | zakilaren gaitza^2 | da
inflammation of penis^1 | is a | disorder of penis^2</td><td>inflamación del pene^1 | es | enfermedad peniana^2
inflammation of penis^1 | is a | disorder of penis^2</td></tr>
<tr><td>zakilaren hantura^1 | zakilaren gaitz^2 | mota bat da
inflammation of penis^1 | is a type of | disorder of penis^2</td><td>trastorno inflamatorio del pene^1 | es un tipo de | enfermedad peniana^2
inflammatory disorder of penis^1 | is a type of | disorder of penis^2</td></tr>
</table>

Table 2: First 10 artificial sentences created from relations in SNOMED CT.

2008 to 2012. Due to privacy agreements, this dissociated corpus is not publicly available.

These documents were first preprocessed to have one sentence in each line, and then the order of the sentences was randomly changed to contribute to a better anonymisation. For making the translation process faster, repeated sentences were removed from the corpus before translating it, resulting in a total of 2,023,811 sentences.

This corpus was added twice to the training corpus, once by applying different backtranslation techniques, and the other by simply using the same corpus in Spanish as if it were Basque (Currey et al., 2017), which we think could be beneficial for the translation of words that do not need to be translated, as it is the case of drug names. This way, from the total number of sentences used for training the corpus based systems developed for translation of clinical texts (9,093,374), around half of them correspond to out-of-domain sentences (4,530,683), and the other half come from diverse clinical domain sources (4,562,691).

Table 3 summarises the numbers of the training corpora. All corpora was tokenised and truecased using the utilities of Nematus (Sennrich et al., 2017) if they were to be used for corpus based systems. For NMT experiments, BPE word segmentation was performed using subword-nmt[2], applying 90,000 merge operations on the joint bilingual corpora. The number of tokens in Basque for the backtranslated EHRs correspond to the backtranslation performed with the shallow RNN.

3.5 EHR templates in Basque and their manual translations into Spanish

For evaluating the task of translating clinical texts, we used 42 EHR templates of diverse specializations written in Basque by doctors of the Donostia Hospital, and their respective manual translations into Spanish carried out by a bilingual doctor. We manually aligned the sentences from these templates with their respective translations, building a bilingual corpus of 2,076 sentences. These sentences were randomly ordered and further divided into 1,038 sentences for development purposes and 1,038 sentences for test purposes.

We highlight that the sentences used for evaluation in the clinical domain come from diverse specializations, which we expect to be mirrored in a more diverse set of development and test corpora. Furthermore, from the 1,038 sentences from the test set, 826 are non-repeated, corresponding the most repeated ones to short sentences relating to EHR section titles. As a sample, Table 4 shows the first 10 sentences used for evaluation in the clinical domain.

4 Experiments

We test our method through two types of experiments, one regarding different NMT architectures, and the other referring to different systems used for backtranslation. All the experiments concerning NMT systems were performed on Titan XP GPUs, using only one for training the shallow RNN, and two for the deep RNN and the Transformer.

4.1 Architectures

First, we test the performance of several neural architectures, trying a shallow RNN as an easily reproducible system, a Transformer (Vaswani et al., 2017) architecture as state-of-the-art performing system, and a deep RNN (Barone et al., 2017) as a fairer comparison to Transformer.

We develop two systems for each architecture, one trained only with out-of-domain corpora, and another trained with all the available resources, including the ones from the clinical domain. For this part of the work, the backtranslation of the available EHRs in Spanish was performed by the shallow RNN.

We evaluate the performance of all the systems in the clinical domain, using the EHR templates in

[2] https://github.com/rsennrich/subword-nmt (Accessed on April 11, 2019.)

Domain	Type	Sentences	Tokens
out-of-domain	Diverse sentences	4.5 million	73 million (Basque) / 102 million (Spanish)
clinical domain	Terms	151,111	271,248 (Basque) / 257,641 (Spanish)
	Artificial sentences	363,958	3.1 million (Basque) / 4.1 million (Spanish)
	Backtranslated EHRs	2 million	26 million (Basque) / 33 million (Spanish)
	Copied EHRs	2 million	33 million

Table 3: Numbers of the training corpora.

Basque sentence	**Spanish sentence**
tratamendua *therapy*	tratamiento *therapy*
abortuak: 1 *aborta 1*	abortos 1 *aborta 1*
lehenengo sintomatologia *first symptomatology*	primera sintomatología *first symptomatology*
fibrinolisiaren ondoren egoera klinikoa ez da askorik aldatu *clinical status does not change much after fibrinolysis*	la situación clínica después de la fibrinólisis no cambia sustancialmente *clinical status after fibrinolysis does not change substantially*
hipertentsioaren aurkako tratamenduarekin hasi da, tentsioak neurri egokian mantenduz; hipergluzemiarako joera antzeman da egonaldian *he/she started the treatment for hypertension, keeping tensions at the right level; a tendency to hyperglycemia is observed during the stay*	al mismo tiempo tratamientopara normalizar la HTA, hiperglucemia y dislipemia *at the same time treatmentfor* normalising HBP, hyperglycemia and dislipemia**
ebakuntza aurreko azterketa normala izan ostean, 2012-08-20an operazioa egin da *after the preoperative examination being normal, the operation is done on 2012-08-20*	tras ser normal la exploración preoperatoria se opera el 20-08-2012, practicándose: *after the preoperative exploration being normal he/she is operated on 2012-08-20, by practising:*
Dismetriarik ez *No dysmetria*	no dismetría *no dysmetria*
miaketa oftalmologikoa normala *normal ophthalmic exploration*	examen oftalmológico normal *normal ophthalmic examination*
EKG: erritmo sinusala, 103 tau/min *ECG: sinus rhythm, 103 beat/min*	EKG-ritmo sinusal 103/minuto *ECG-sinus rhythm, 103/min*
ez du botaka egin *he/she has not vomited*	no vómitos *no vomits*

Table 4: First 10 sentences used for evaluation in the clinical domain.

Basque and their manual translations into Spanish specified in the previous section.

A description of the tested architectures is given in the following lines.

Shallow RNN: As a simple RNN, we use a model developed with the old version of Nematus (Sennrich et al., 2017), making use of the Theano framework. Specifically, we use 1 layer (bidirectional for the encoder) of 1024 GRU (Cho et al., 2014) units, with a embedding-size of 500, a batch-size of 64 and using Adam (Kingma and Ba, 2014) as optimisation method. For decoding, we use a beam-width of 10 for all the experiments. Some of the values of these hyperparameters were optimised with the out-of-domain corpus, and subsequently used in the other architectures.

Deep RNN: As a more advanced RNN, we select the system developed by Barone et al. (2017), included in a more recent work in which linguistic abilities of diverse NMT systems were tested (Tang et al., 2018).

From the different variants presented in Barone et al. (2017), we use the one that obtained the best reported results, whose configuration parameters are public.[3]

Transformer: As a state-of-the-art NMT system, we choose the Transformer implementation in Pytorch by OpenNMT (Klein et al., 2017). We use the recommended hyperparameters,[4] except for the number of GPUs and batch-size, that were

[3] `https://github.com/Avmb/deep-nmt-architectures/blob/master/configs/bideep-bideep-rGRU-large/config.sh` (Accessed on April 11, 2019.)

[4] `http://opennmt.net/OpenNMT-py/FAQ.html#how-do-i-use-the-transformer-model-do-you-support-multi-gpu` (Accessed on April 11, 2019.)

halved to meet our hardware capabilities.

4.2 Backtranslation systems

After trying different architectures, we select the one that obtains the best automatic evaluation results in the clinical domain and change the way the backtranslation is performed. For that, we compare the shallow RNN architecture with the one that gets the best results in the clinical domain, and also try RBMT and SMT systems to translate the EHRs in Spanish into Basque.

For training the corpus based systems in the Spanish-to-Basque translation direction, we use the out-of-domain corpus and the dictionaries including clinical terminology. The resulting synthetic corpus is added together with the artificial sentences and the copied monolingual corpus, and the performance of the systems is tested in the clinical domain.

Shallow RNN: For this experiment we use the same shallow RNN architecture specified in the previous section, just changing the translation direction. Note that, due to an error in the preprocessing, the BPE word segmentation was performed for 45,000 steps in each language corpus, instead of 90,000 times in the joint corpora. We do not expect for this error to have significant influence on the final results.

Transformer: We train the Transformer system in the Spanish-to-Basque translation direction with the same hyperparameters specified in the previous section. Following the work by Edunov et al. (2018), we perform the translation by unrestricted random sampling, which is proved to obtain better results than restricted random sampling or traditional beam search when applied to backtranslation.

RBMT: For this part of the work, we try Matxin (Mayor, 2007), a Rule-Based system for Spanish-to-Basque Machine Translation, adapted to the biomedical domain by the inclusion of dictionaries. In this case, we translate the EHRs in Spanish before truecasing, so when removing the repeated sentences from the corpora the number of sentences is not exactly the same as for the monolingual corpus translated with corpus based systems (2,036,165 instead of 2,023,811).

SMT: Finally, we try Moses (Koehn et al., 2007) as a statistical system, adapted to the biomedical domain. We use default parametrisation with MGIZA for word alignment, a "msd-bidirectional-fe" lexicalised reordering model and a KenLM (Heafield, 2011) 5-gram target language model. The weights for the different components were adjusted to optimise BLEU using Minimum Error Rate Training (MERT) with an n-best list of size 100.

5 Results and discussion

In this section we show and discuss the automatic evaluation results of the experiments carried out with different architectures and backtranslation systems. In both cases, we calculate BLEU (Papineni et al., 2002) in development and test sets using the multi-bleu script included in Moses.[5]

5.1 Architectures

Table 5 shows the results of the tested architectures in two variants: 1) trained only with out-of-domain corpora, and 2) including all the clinical domain resources. We observe large and consistent improvements when adding in-domain data to each of the tested architectures. Surprisingly, the deep RNN obtains lower results than the shallow RNN, especially comparing the systems trained out-of-domain, which can be an overfitting issue. We also think that the previous optimisation with the out-of-domain corpus of some of the hyperparameters of the shallow RNN can be a reason for its good results, comparable with Transformer regarding the systems trained only with out-of-domain corpora, and similar to deep RNN when adding the clinical domain resources.

	dev	test
Shallow RNN (out-of-domain)	10.69	10.67
Shallow RNN (+in-domain)	23.57	21.59
Deep RNN (out-of-domain)	7.23	5.91
Deep RNN (+in-domain)	23.01	20.74
Transformer (out-of-domain)	10.92	10.55
Transformer (+in-domain)	**26.67**	**24.44**

Table 5: BLEU values (Basque-to-Spanish) for different architectures using a shallow RNN for backtranslation.

However, if we compare the results of the different architectures trained with all the available re-

[5] `https://github.com/moses-smt/mosesdecoder/blob/master/scripts/generic/multi-bleu.perl` (Accessed on April 11, 2019.)

sources, we see that Transformer outperforms both RNNs by around 3 BLEU points in each evaluation set. Thus, we can say that the Transformer architecture is the optimal for our task of translating clinical texts from Basque to Spanish.

5.2 Backtranslation systems

After determining which is the best general architecture for our task, we compare the results of different backtranslation systems. First, we evaluate the performance of the systems used to translate the available EHRs in Spanish into Basque, using as a reference the same datasets employed for evaluating the different architectures. Table 6 shows the results of the tested backtranslation systems.

	dev	test
$RBMT_{bt}$	8.56	7.03
SMT_{bt}	10.30	8.75
Shallow RNN_{bt}	10.75	10.44
$Transformer_{bt}$	**11.30**	**12.04**

Table 6: BLEU values for different backtranslation systems (Spanish-to-Basque).

We observe that the values obtained with NMT systems are similar to the ones obtained in the other direction with the system trained out-of-domain, which is logical since we only added the dictionaries for training the backtranslation systems. The results of SMT are also similar, with a slightly lower score in the test set. The results for RBMT are even lower, which can be because BLEU underestimates the results of RBMT systems in general.

Finally, we present in Table 7 the results in the clinical domain of the systems trained with the best performing architecture (Transformer) using all the training corpora, changing the method used for backtranslating the EHRs in Spanish.

	dev	test
RBMT	22.98	21.91
SMT	22.78	21.43
Shallow RNN	26.67	24.44
Transformer	**27.70**	**25.61**

Table 7: BLEU values (Basque-to-Spanish) for Transformer architecture using different backtranslation systems.

We notice that using Transformer for backtranslation obtains the best results, gaining more than 1 BLEU point comparing with the same Transformer architecture using a shallow RNN for backtranslation. The results for RBMT and SMT are lower, but comparing to the BLEU values for the backtranslation systems (Table 6), we observe that in this case the results using RBMT are slightly better than the ones with SMT. Apart from the aforementioned possible underestimation of RBMT systems when calculating BLEU, we think that this could be because the RBMT system can translate words that corpus based systems cannot translate, adding more variability to the source language corpus.

5.3 Ensemble of best models

After evaluating the performance of different architectures and backtranslation systems, we evaluate the performance of an ensemble of the 3 systems obtaining highest BLEU values in the development set, which in this case correspond to 3 different models of the Transformer architecture, using Transformer as backtranslation system, saved after different number of iterations. Specifically, the models evaluated for the ensemble are those saved after 90,000, 160,000 and 180,000 iterations, obtaining 27.56 BLEU points with the first two models, and 27.70 BLEU points with the last one. Table 8 shows the results of the ensemble system, which we name IxaMedNMT-Transformer. We observe gains of 0.33 BLEU points in the development set and 0.11 BLEU points in the test set, comparing to the results of the single model that obtained the highest BLEU value in the development set.

	dev	test
IxaMedNMT-Transformer	28.03	25.72

Table 8: BLEU values (Basque-to-Spanish) for an ensemble of the best performing systems.

5.4 Translation example and error analysis

Finally, Figure 1 shows an example of a translation performed by the ensemble system whose BLEU values were shown in Table 8, along with the original sentence in Basque and the manual translation into Spanish used as a reference.

We observe that the generated translation is almost equivalent to the human translation, with only slight differences in some of the words (presents/with, complete/wide, stenoses/obstructs, part/region, etc.), but without changing the overall meaning of the original sentence in Basque.

Original sentence in Basque

azaleko izter-arteria-k buxadura zabala du, baina iragazkor dago Hunter-en eremu-raino,
superficial femoral artery-ERG obstruction wide has, but permeable is Hunter-GEN region-ALL,
'the superficial femoral artery has a wide obstruction, but it is permeable up to the Hunter region,...

bertan buxatu eta 3. eremu popliteo-an berriz ere iragazkor bihurtzen da.
there obstruct and 3rd region popliteal-LOC again also permeable becoming is.
it is obstructed there and becomes permeable again in the 3rd popliteal region.'

Manual translation into Spanish

arteria femoral superficial con estenosis amplia pero permeable hasta la zona de Hunter
artery femoral superficial with stenosis wide but permeable up-to the region of Hunter
'superficial femoral artery with wide obstruction but permeable up to the Hunter region...

donde se estenosa, y en la zona 3 poplítea se vuelve otra vez permeable.
where it stenoses, and in the region 3 popliteal it becomes another.F time permeable.

where it stenoses and becomes permeable again in the popliteal region 3.'

Translation by the IxaMedNMT-Transformer system

la arteria femoral superficial presenta una oclusión completa que se encuentra permeable hasta el
the artery femoral superficial presents a occlusion complete which is found permeable up-to the
'the superficial femoral artery presents a complete occlusion which is permeable up to the...

área de Hunter, donde se obstruye y se vuelve permeable en la 3ª porción poplítea.
region of Hunter, where it obstructs and it becomes permeable in the 3rd portion popliteal.

Hunter region, where it is obstructed and becomes permeable in the 3rd popliteal portion.'

Figure 1: Translation example by the IxaMedNMT-Transformer system, along with the original sentence in Basque and the manual translation into Spanish.

In a fast overview of the whole of the sentences translated from the development set, we have observed that for some of the long sentences, the translation ended abruptly without translating a few of the last words. We have tried to scale down the beam-width from 10 (optimised for the shallow RNN, kept in other architectures for fair comparison) to the default value of 5 to reduce the probability of generating the end-of-sentence token sooner than necessary, but the BLEU values in the development set did not improve as expected. We plan to test diverse values of length-normalisation and coverage-penalty coefficients to try to overcome this problem.

This phenomenon occurred especially in sentences with a lot of punctuation marks, usually containing a list of symptoms, diseases or drugs. Regarding the translation of rare words, like in this case drug names, we have observed very few errors where part of the word was not translated correctly due to the BPE word segmentation. In the future, we intend to perform a thorough analysis of the different types of errors encountered in the generated translations, with the aim of developing possible solutions to them.

6 Conclusions and future work

We have showed that it is possible to translate clinical texts from Basque to Spanish without clinical domain bilingual corpora. We have leveraged previous work in translation of clinical terminology into Basque (Perez-de-Viñaspre, 2017), described a method for creating artificial sentences based on SNOMED CT relations, and made use of available EHRs in Spanish. Given the multilinguality and rich structure of SNOMED CT, similar dictionaries and artificial sentences might be generated for other language pairs for which bilingual clinical corpora are not available.

Furthermore, we have tested our method with different NMT architectures and using diverse systems for backtranslation, including rule-based and statistical systems. We obtained the best results using Transformer for both general architecture and backtranslation systems, achieving 28 BLEU points in the development set through checkpoint ensembling, and showing a translation example.

We leave as future work the human evaluation of the best performing system, with the possibility of improving the corpora used for training and evaluation.

Acknowledgements: This work was supported by the Spanish Ministry of Economy and Competitiveness (MINECO) FPI grant number BES-2017-081045, and projects BigKnowledge (BBVA foundation grant 2018), DOMINO (PGC2018-102041-B-I00, MCIU/AEI/FEDER, UE) and PROSA-MED (TIN2016-77820-C3-1-R, MCIU/AEI/FEDER, UE). We thank Uxoa Iñurrieta for helping us with the glosses.

References

Agirre, Eneko, Inaki Alegria, Xabier Arregi, Xabier Artola, Arantza Díaz de Ilarraza, Montse Maritxalar, Kepa Sarasola, and Miriam Urkia. 1992. XUXEN: A spelling checker/corrector for Basque based on Two-Level morphology. In *Proceedings of the third conference on Applied natural language processing*, 119–125.

Alegria, Iñaki, Xabier Artola, Kepa Sarasola, and Miriam Urkia. 1996. Automatic morphological analysis of Basque. *Literary and Linguistic Computing*, 11(4):193–203.

Ataman, Duygu, Matteo Negri, Marco Turchi, and Marcello Federico. 2017. Linguistically Motivated Vocabulary Reduction for Neural Machine Translation from Turkish to English. *The Prague Bulletin of Mathematical Linguistics*, 108:331–342.

Bapna, Ankur, and Orhan Firat. 2019. Non-Parametric Adaptation for Neural Machine Translation. *arXiv preprint arXiv:1903.00058*

Barone, Antonio Valerio Miceli, Jindřich Helcl, Rico Sennrich, Barry Haddow, and Alexandra Birch. 2017. Deep architectures for neural machine translation. *arXiv preprint arXiv:1707.07631*

Burlot, Franck, and François Yvon. 2019. Using Monolingual Data in Neural Machine Translation: a Systematic Study. *arXiv preprint arXiv:1903.11437*

Cho, Kyunghyun, Bart Van Merriënboer, Caglar Gulcehre, Dzmitry Bahdanau, Fethi Bougares, Holger Schwenk, and Yoshua Bengio. 2014. Learning phrase representations using RNN encoder-decoder for statistical machine translation. *arXiv preprint arXiv:1406.1078*

Currey, Anna, Antonio Valerio Miceli Barone, and Kenneth Heafield. 2017. Copied monolingual data improves low-resource neural machine translation. In *Proceedings of the Second Conference on Machine Translation*, 148–156.

Edunov, Sergey, Myle Ott, Michael Auli, and David Grangier. 2018. Understanding back-translation at scale. *arXiv preprint arXiv:1808.09381*

Etchegoyhen, Thierry, Andoni Azpeitia, and Naiara Pérez. 2016. Exploiting a Large Strongly Comparable Corpus. In *Proceedings of the Tenth International Conference on Language Resources and Evaluation (LREC 2016)*, Porotoroz, Slovenia.

Etchegoyhen, Thierry, Eva Martínez, Andoni Azpeitia, Gorka Labaka, Iñaki Alegria, Itziar Cortes, Amaia Jauregi, Igor Ellakuria, Maite Martin and Eusebi Calonge. 2018. Neural Machine Translation of Basque. *Proceedings of the 21st Annual Conference of the European Association for Machine Translation*, Alacant, Spain, 139–148.

Heafield, Kenneth. 2011. KenLM: Faster and Smaller Language Model Queries. In *Proceedings of the Sixth Workshop on Statistical Machine Translation*, 187–197.

Hochreiter, Sepp, and Jürgen Schmidhuber. 1997. Long short-term memory. *Neural computation*, 9(8):1735–1780.

International Health Terminology Standards Development Organisation IHTSDO. 2014. *SNOMED CT Starter Guide*. Technical report, International Health Terminology Standards Development Organisation

Jauregi, Inigo, Lierni Garmendia, Ehsan Zare, and Massimo Piccardi. 2018. English-Basque statistical and neural machine translation. In *Proceedings of the Eleventh International Conference on Language Resources and Evaluation*, 880–885.

Joanes Etxeberri Saria V. Edizioa. 2014. *Donostia Unibertsitate Ospitaleko alta-txostenak*. Donostiako Unibertsitate Ospitalea, Komunikazio Unitatea

Kalchbrenner, Nal, and Phil Blunsom. 2013. Recurrent continuous translation models. In *Proceedings of the 2013 Conference on Empirical Methods in Natural Language Processing*, 1700–1709.

Kingma, Diederik P., and Jimmy Ba. 2014. Adam: A method for stochastic optimization. *arXiv preprint arXiv:1412.6980*

Klein, Guillaume, Yoon Kim, Yuntian Deng, Jean Senellart, and Alexander M. Rush. 2017. Opennmt: Open-source toolkit for neural machine translation. *arXiv preprint arXiv:1701.02810*

Koehn, Philipp, Franz Josef Och, and Daniel Marcu. 2003. Statistical phrase-based translation. In *Proceedings of the 2003 Conference of the North American Chapter of the Association for Computational Linguistics on Human Language Technology-Volume 1*, 48–54.

Koehn, Philipp, Hieu Hoang, Alexandra Birch, Chris Callison-Burch, Marcello Federico, Nicola Bertoldi, Brooke Cowan, Wade Shen, Christine Moran, Richard Zens, Chris Dyer, Ondřej Bojar, Alexandra Constantin and Evan Herbst. 2007. Moses: Open source toolkit for statistical machine translation. In

Proceedings of the 45th annual meeting of the association for computational linguistics companion volume proceedings of the demo and poster sessions, 177–180.

Koehn, Philipp, and Rebecca Knowles. 2017. Six challenges for neural machine translation. *arXiv preprint arXiv:1706.03872*

Labaka, Gorka. 2010. *EUSMT: incorporating linguistic information into SMT for a morphologically rich language. Its use in SMT-RBMT-EBMT hybridation.*. PhD thesis, University of the Basque Country, Donostia, Euskal Herria.

Lee, Jason, Kyunghyun Cho, and Thomas Hofmann. 2016. Fully character-level neural machine translation without explicit segmentation. *arXiv preprint arXiv:1610.03017*

Liu, Weisong, and Shu Cai. 2015. Translating electronic health record notes from English to Spanish: A preliminary study. *Proceedings of BioNLP 15*, 139–148.

Mayor, Aingeru. 2007. *Erregeletan oinarritutako itzulpen automatikoko sistema baten eraikuntza estaldura handiko baliabide linguistikoak berrerabiliz.*. PhD thesis, University of the Basque Country, Donostia, Euskal Herria.

Otegi, Arantxa, Nerea Ezeiza, Iakes Goenaga, and Gorka Labaka. 2016. A Modular Chain of NLP Tools for Basque, 93–100.

Papineni, Kishore, Salim Roukos, Todd Ward, and Wei-Jing Zhu. 2002. BLEU: a method for automatic evaluation of machine translation. In *Proceedings of the 40th annual meeting on association for computational linguistics*, 311–318.

Perez-de-Viñaspre, Olatz. 2017. *Automatic medical term generation for a low-resource language: translation of SNOMED CT into Basque*. PhD thesis, University of the Basque Country, Donostia, Euskal Herria.

Poncelas, Alberto, Dimitar Shterionov, Andy Way, Gideon Maillette de Buy Wenniger, and Peyman Passban. 2018. Investigating backtranslation in neural machine translation. *arXiv preprint arXiv:1804.06189*

Sennrich, Rico, Barry Haddow, and Alexandra Birch. 2015. Improving neural machine translation models with monolingual data. *arXiv preprint arXiv:1511.06709*

Sennrich, Rico, Barry Haddow, and Alexandra Birch. 2015. Neural machine translation of rare words with subword units. *arXiv preprint arXiv:1508.07909*

Sennrich, Rico, Orhan Firat, Kyunghyun Cho, Alexandra Birch, Barry Haddow, Julian Hitschler, Marcin Junczys-Dowmunt, Samuel Läubli, Antonio Valerio Miceli Barone, Jozef Mokry, and Maria Nădejde. 2017. Nematus: a toolkit for neural machine translation. *arXiv preprint arXiv:1703.04357*

Stroppa, Nicolas, Decan Groves, Andy Way, and Kepa Sarasola. 2006. Example-based machine translation of the basque language. In *Proceedings of the 7th Conference of the Association for Machine Translation in the Americas*, Cambridge, MA USA, 232–241.

Sutskever, Ilya, Oriol Vinyals, and Quoc V. Le. 2014. Sequence to sequence learning with neural networks. In *Advances in neural information processing systems*, 3104–3112.

Tang, Gongbo, Mathias Müller, Annette Rios, and Rico Sennrich. 2018. Why self-attention? a targeted evaluation of neural machine translation architectures. *arXiv preprint arXiv:1808.08946*

Vaswani, Ashish, Noam Shazeer, Niki Parmar, Jakob Uszkoreit, Llion Jones, Aidan N. Gomez, Łukasz Kaiser, and Illia Polosukhin. 2017. Attention is all you need. In *Advances in Neural Information Processing Systems*, 5998–6008.

Zeiler, Matthew D. 2012. ADADELTA: an adaptive learning rate method. *arXiv preprint arXiv:1212.5701*

Zoph, Barret, Deniz Yuret, Jonathan May, and Kevin Knight. 2016. Transfer learning for low-resource neural machine translation. *arXiv preprint arXiv:1604.02201*

Author Index

Association for Computational Linguistics
209 N. Eighth Street
Stroudsburg, Pennsylvania 18360

ISBN 978-1-5108-9249-1

CURRAN ASSOCIATES INC.
proceedings.com